T0198741

The Adventures of God's Team

God's Number Book 1-12

Written by
Sevina

Illustrations by Catherine Harrison age 10
Graphic design by Jan Reid

WestBow Press books may be ordered through booksellers or by contacting:

WestBow Press
A Division of Thomas Nelson & Zondervan
1663 Liberty Drive
Bloomington, IN 47403
www.westbowpress.com
1 (866) 928-1240

Illustrations by Catherine Harrison age 10
Graphic design by Jan Reid

Scripture quotations taken from The Holy Bible, New International Version® NIV® Copyright ©
1973, 1978, 1984, 2011 by Biblica, Inc. TM. Used by permission. All rights reserved worldwide.

ISBN: 978-1-9736-7943-1 (sc)
ISBN: 978-1-9736-7944-8 (e)

Library of Congress Control Number: 2019918044

Print information available on the last page.

WestBow Press rev. date: 05/29/2020

WestBow
PRESS®
A DIVISION OF THOMAS NELSON
& ZONDERVAN

Note to Parents/Guardians of the children being read to:

Due to the vast age of the child this book is intended for, which can be as young as toddlers, I would like to recommend a few suggestions.

First, I would like to suggest that the reader simply read the numbers and count the items on each page for the very young toddler. At this stage of their development, the child will only be able to comprehend the counting of the objects and stating what each object is. As they grow, you can add the bible verse when you feel it best to do so.

Second, a school age child can become acclimated to the bible verse as each page is being read. Elementary age children may even want a further explanation of the bible verse and it would be convenient to have a bible on hand to read the portion of the bible the verse is from. Your expertise can further explain the verse as it relates to the bible story.

However, for those parent/guardians that are fairly new to our wonderful Christian world and God's glorious Bible, here are suggestions for each bible verse explanation:

One God: There is only one Supreme Being, the one that created everything, and that is God our Father.

Two Turtle Doves: These were given as offerings when Jesus was brought to Jerusalem for his ceremony of purification 40 days after he was born.

Three: The Holy Trinity: Jesus told his disciples to go into the world and baptize all people in the name of the Father and of the Son and of the Holy Spirit. The Father is God, the Son is Jesus and the Holy Spirit is our helper sent by Jesus after he rose to heaven.

Four rings of gold: These rings, two on each side, were on the ark that was built to be a holy place where God would meet and speak with Moses.

Five Smooth Stones: David put these five stones in his pouch and used one of them to kill Goliath with a sling.

Six water pots: Jesus turned these six pots of water into wine at a wedding he was attending, which was a miracle to show the power and glory of Jesus.

Seven churches: At the time of Jesus' death, there were seven churches in Asia and after the writings of what Jesus did were complete, it was to be sent to these seven churches.

Eight souls saved: These were the people in Noah's Ark that were saved, Noah and his wife, and his three sons and their wives.

Nine fruits of the Holy Spirit: The Holy Spirit produces in us these nine virtues. We do not create them ourselves; they are given to us from the Holy Spirit.

Ten Commandments:

1. You shall have no other gods but God our Father
2. You shall not have any idols
3. You shall not take God's name in vain
4. You shall keep the Sabbath day Holy with no work
5. You shall honor your father and mother
6. You shall not kill
7. You shall not commit adultery
8. You shall not steal
9. You shall not bear false witness (do not lie)
10. You shall not desire your neighbor's things

Eleven Curtains of the Tabernacle: These curtains were made to protect the more expensive curtains below these when building the tabernacle, which was a place of worship constructed by Moses.

Twelve Apostles: These were the original twelve men Jesus chose to be with Him. Their names were Peter, James the son of Zebedee, John, Andrew, Philip, Bartholomew, Matthew, Thomas, James the son of Alphaeus, Thaddaeus, Simon and Judas.

Enjoy learning about God's numbers 1-12!

"Hey everyone, I just got word from God that he wants us to write a number book for the little children," yelled Tech-mania Miles.

"We better put our thinking caps on and get started," said Monster Truck Ethan as he started revving up his engines for this mission.

Enchanting Emma called out, "LET'S PRAY ... and let's get to work!"

God

NIV 1 Timothy 2:5 "For there is one God ..."

Turtledoves

NIV Luke 2:24 "... a pair of turtle doves ..."

Holy Trinity

NIV Matthew 28:19 "... baptizing them in the name of the
Father and of the Son and of the Holy Spirit..."

Rings of Gold

NIV Exodus 25:12 "You shall cast four rings of gold for it..."

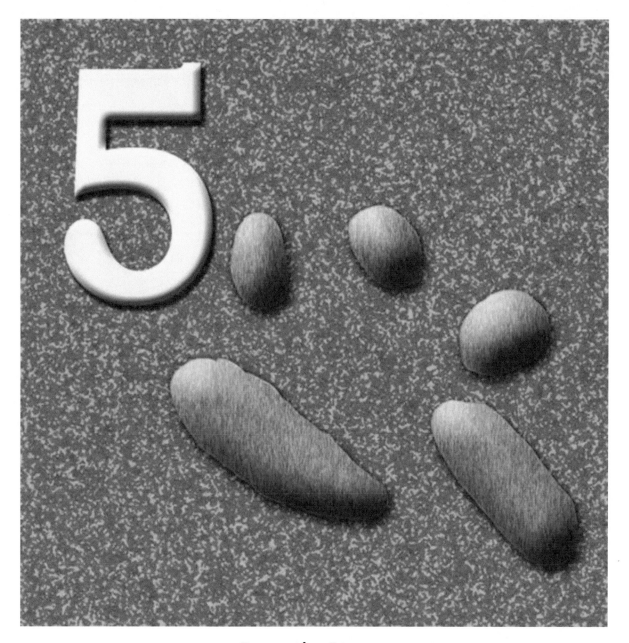

Smooth Stones

NIV 1 Samuel 17:40 "...and he chose for himself
five smooth stones from the brook..."

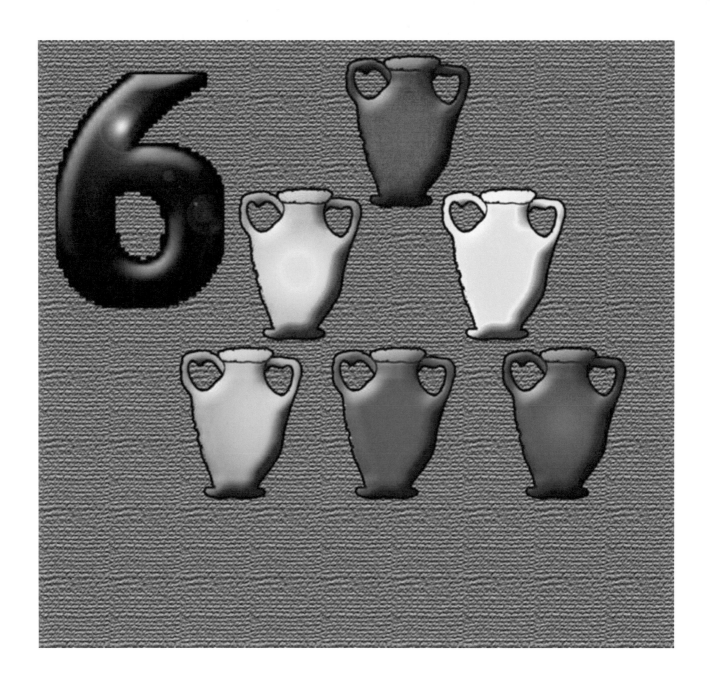

Water Pots

NIV John 2:6 "Now there were set there six water pots of stone ..."

Churches

NIV Revelations 1:11 "... and send it to the
seven churches which are in Asia..."

Souls Saved

NIV 1 Peter 3:20 "...eight souls were saved through water."

Fruits of the Holy Spirit

NIV Galatians 5:22-23 "...But the fruit of the Spirit is love, joy, peace, longsuffering, kindness, goodness, faithfulness, gentleness, self-control..."

The Ten Commandments

NIV Exodus 20: 1-17

Curtains of the Tabernacle

NIV Exodus 26:7 "... You shall make eleven curtains."

Apostles

NIV Mark 3:14 "Then He appointed twelve, that they might be with Him…"

The team was very glad they listened to God cause
that made writing the book much easier.

As in NIV Isaiah 28:26 it says,

"For He instructs him in right judgment, his God teaches him."

And God's Team was very happy to finish yet another mission for God!

Printed in the United States
By Bookmasters